SPORTS SUPERSTARS

I0878824

WHO IS SIMONE BILES?

ZELDA WAGNER

Lerner Publications ◆ Minneapolis

Copyright © 2026 by Lerner Publishing Group, Inc.

Statistics in this book are accurate through June 1, 2025.

All rights reserved. International copyright secured. No part of this book may be reproduced, stored in a retrieval system, or transmitted in any form or by any means—electronic, mechanical, photocopying, recording, or otherwise—without the prior written permission of Lerner Publishing Group, Inc., except for the inclusion of brief quotations in an acknowledged review.

Lerner Publications Company
An imprint of Lerner Publishing Group, Inc.
241 First Avenue North
Minneapolis, MN 55401 USA

For reading levels and more information, look up this title at www.lernerbooks.com.

Main body text set in Mikado.
Typeface provided by HvD Fonts.

Editor: Annie Zheng **Designer:** Mary Ross

Library of Congress Cataloging-in-Publication Data

Names: Wagner, Zelda, 2000- author.
Title: Who is Simone Biles? : USA gymnastics superstar / Zelda Wagner.
Description: Minneapolis, MN : Lerner Publications, 2026. | Series: Sports superstars (Lerner Sports Rookie) | Includes bibliographical references and index. | Audience: Ages 5–8 | Audience: Grades K–1 | Summary: "Simone Biles is the greatest gymnast of all time. She has 11 Olympic and 30 World Championship medals. Readers will discover more about her life and career"— Provided by publisher.
Identifiers: LCCN 2025017525 (print) | LCCN 2025017526 (ebook) | ISBN 9798765689608 (library binding) | ISBN 9798348029104 (paperback) | ISBN 9798765697825 (epub)
Subjects: LCSH: Biles, Simone 1997- —Juvenile literature. | Olympic athletes—United States—Biography—Juvenile literature. | Women gymnasts—United States—Biography—Juvenile literature. | African American women athletes—United States—Biography—Juvenile literature. | African American women Olympic athletes—United States—Biography—Juvenile literature.
Classification: LCC GV460.2.B55 W346 2026 (print) | LCC GV460.2.B55 (ebook) | DDC 796.44092 [B]—dc23/eng/20250621

LC record available at https://lccn.loc.gov/2025017525
LC ebook record available at https://lccn.loc.gov/2025017526

Manufactured in the United States of America
1-1012761-54828-6/24/2025

TABLE OF CONTENTS

A WORLD CHAMPION

Simone Biles ran toward the vaulting table at the 2024 Olympics. She pushed off the table and did two flips in the air.

Simone earned a final score of 15.3. She won the gold medal for vault!

Simone was born on March 14, 1997, in Columbus, Ohio.

She joined a gymnastics club
when she was six years old.

Simone was a natural. She was better than other gymnasts her age.

When she was 16, she won her first gold medal at a world event.

Simone stood out from other gymnasts. She did moves that they couldn't match.

In 2016, she competed at the Olympics in Brazil.

She took home four gold medals and one bronze medal.

Her success made her a fan favorite. People around the world cheered for her.

At the 2020 Olympics in Japan, Simone won a silver medal and a bronze medal.

But she soon withdrew from the Olympics to focus on her mental health.

For two years, Simone did not compete. Then, in 2023, she returned to the sport.

She won big at the US Classic in Illinois. She took home three gold medals and one bronze medal.

She also won four gold medals and a silver medal at the World Championships.

Simone made it back to the Olympics in 2024 in France. She showed that she was still the best gymnast in the world.

She took home three gold medals and one silver medal.

Simone has already won 11 Olympic medals. She hopes to add more medals in 2028. With Simone, anything is possible!

SIMONE BILES

CAREER STATS

OLYMPIC MEDALS: 11

WORLD CHAMPIONSHIP MEDALS: 30

US CHAMPIONSHIP MEDALS: 41

US CLASSIC MEDALS: 26

SIMONE BILES

GEAR

GLOSSARY

mental health: the state of being happy and healthy

vault: when a gymnast launches from a vaulting table into the air

vaulting table: a piece of equipment that a gymnast launches from

LEARN MORE

Hansen, Grace. *Simone Biles.* Abdo Kids Jumbo, 2022.

Rose, Rachel. *Simone Biles: Gymnastics Superstar.* Bearport, 2023.

Wagner, Zelda. *Gymnastics Superstars.* Lerner Publications, 2025.

INDEX

PHOTO ACKNOWLEDGMENTS

Image credits: Julian Finney/Getty Images, p. 5; Richard I'Anson/Getty Images, p. 6; Smiley N. Pool/Houston Chronicle/Getty Images, p. 8; Alex Livesey/Getty Images, p. 10; Amin Mohammad Jamali/Getty Images, p. 12; EMMANUEL DUNAND/AF/Getty Images, p. 14; Tim Clayton/Corbis/Getty Images, p. 17; Jamie Squire/Getty Images, p. 19; Jamie Squire/Getty Images, p. 21; KEREM YUCEL/AFP/Getty Images, p. 23; Design element: liangpv/Getty Images.
Cover: AP Photo/David G. McIntyre.